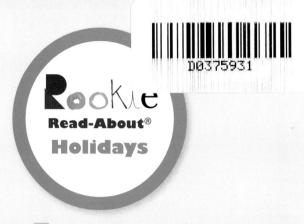

Christmas

by Trudi Strain Trueit

Content Consultants

Nanci R. Vargus, Ed.D.
Professor Emeritus, University of Indianapolis

Carrie A. Bell, MST Visual Arts – All Grades
Julia A. Stark Elementary School, Stamford, Connecticut

Reading Consultant

Jeanne M. Clidas, Ph.D.
Reading Specialist

Children's Press®
An Imprint of Scholastic Inc.
New York Toronto London Auckland Sydney
Mexico City New Delhi Hong Kong
Danbury, Connecticut

Library of Congress Cataloging-in-Publication Data
Trueit, Trudi Strain.
  Christmas / by Trudi Strain Trueit.
    pages cm. — (Rookie read-about holidays)
  Includes index.
  ISBN 978-0-531-27202-2 (library binding) — ISBN 978-0-531-27352-4 (pbk.)
  1. Christmas—Juvenile literature. I. Title.

GT4985.5.T78 2013
394.2663—dc23   2013014834

Produced by Spooky Cheetah Press

Printed in China 62

SCHOLASTIC, CHILDREN'S PRESS, ROOKIE READ-ABOUT®, and associated logos
are trademarks and/or registered trademarks of Scholastic Inc.

1 2 3 4 5 6 7 8 9 10 R 23 22 21 20 19 18 17 16 15 14

Photographs © 2014: Adam Chinitz: 28; Alamy Images/Cindy Hopkins: 4, 31 top;
Getty Images: 20 (Luke Stettner), 12 (The Bridgeman Art Library); iStockphoto/
RonTech2000: 23, 32 bottom; Louise Gardner: 7; Media Bakery: 8, 27 (Blend
Images), 16; PhotoEdit/Michael Newman: 30 left; Shutterstock, Inc.: 19 (Andresr),
cover (Sebastian Kaulitzki); Superstock, Inc.: 15, 30 right, 31 center bottom (Belinda
Images), 24 (FELLOW), 11 (imagebroker.net), 31 center top; Thinkstock/iStockphoto: 3
top, 3 bottom.

Table of Contents

Joy to the World

See the lights twinkle on the tree.
Touch the pretty **ornaments**.
Taste the warm gingerbread.
Hear the people sing **carols**.
It is Christmastime!

This group is singing
Christmas carols.

5

Christmas is December 25th. People in more than 160 countries celebrate this holiday. In the United States, children have the day off from school.

Christmas is celebrated on the same date every year.

DECEMBER

SUNDAY	MONDAY	TUESDAY	WEDNESDAY	THURSDAY	FRIDAY	SATURDAY
	1	2	3	4	5	6
7	8	9	10	11	12	13
14	15	16	17	18	19	20
21	22	23	24	25	26	27
28	29	30	31			

Christmas celebrates the birth of Jesus Christ. Some people, called Christians, believe that Jesus Christ is the son of God.

Christmas is also a time to share with others. It is a holiday of peace and joy.

Christmas is a time to be with loved ones.

How It Began

Long ago, winter **festivals** were common in Rome. Christians in Rome decided to celebrate the birth of Jesus Christ. Since no one knew Jesus's true birthday, they made the birthday celebration part of the winter festival.

This decoration, called a crèche (kresh), shows the birth of Jesus.

In time, people began to call the holiday Christmas. Christmas continued to be celebrated throughout history and in countries around the world.

FAST FACT!

Christmas means "festival of Christ."

Getting in the Spirit

An early Christmas **tradition** was to put up a tree. A church leader in Germany put candles on his tree. His name was Martin Luther. These were some of the first Christmas lights!

15

Giving gifts has always been part of the holiday. Christians believe Jesus got the first gifts when he was born.

This girl got a puppy for Christmas!

Early on, children in Europe were given small gifts, such as fruit, candy, and toys. Some of their gifts came from their families. Some came from Saint Nicholas. In the United States, Saint Nicholas was called Santa Claus.

FAST FACT!

Candy canes are a traditional Christmas candy. The first ones were all white and did not have a hook!

19

Merry Christmas!

Today we celebrate Christmas in different ways. Many people decorate a tree with lights and ornaments. Some also decorate the outside of their houses.

FAST FACT!

About 35 million Christmas trees are sold in the United States each year.

Many people have other fun Christmas traditions. They may bake cookies and build gingerbread houses. They may send Christmas cards to family and friends.

This family is making a gingerbread house together.

24

Some people go to church on Christmas Eve. That is the night before Christmas. They hear the story of Jesus's birth. They light candles. They say prayers. They sing "Silent Night" and other carols.

These children are singing in a church choir. They are dressed as angels.

Santa Claus makes his visit on Christmas Eve. He comes while everyone is asleep. Children hang stockings for Santa Claus to fill with gifts. They find the gifts on Christmas morning and say, "Merry Christmas!"

It looks like these kids are having a very merry Christmas!

Make Santa's Reindeer

What You'll Need

- Pencil
- Dark brown, tan, and red construction paper
- Scissors
- Glue

- Crayons
- Googly eyes (optional)
- Small red or brown pompom (optional)

Directions

1. Use the pencil to trace your foot on the brown construction paper. This will be your reindeer's face. Trace both of your hands on the tan construction paper. These will be the reindeer's antlers.

2. With an adult's help, cut out the prints. Cut a circle from the red paper to make a nose.

3. To create your reindeer, glue the handprints to the top of the footprint. Draw on eyes and a mouth. Glue on the nose. Or glue on googly eyes for the reindeer's eyes and a pompom for its nose.

Show What You Know!

A Very Special Day

Christmas traditions are things that people do year after year. They make the season special. One tradition might be making a gingerbread house. Another might be visiting your grandparents.

- Which of these photos shows a Christmas tradition? Why?
- Does your family have any Christmas traditions? What are they?
- Ask your parents to share traditions from when they were young.

Glossary

carols (KAR-uhls): traditional Christmas songs

festivals (FESS-tuh-vuhls): celebrations

ornaments (OR-nuh-muhnts): balls, stars, and other Christmas tree decorations

tradition (truh-DIH-shun): a custom that is handed down from parents to children

Index

Facts for Now

Visit this Scholastic Web site for more information on Christmas:
www.factsfornow.scholastic.com
Enter the keyword **Christmas**

About the Author

Trudi Strain Trueit has written more than 80 fiction and nonfiction books for children. She was born and raised and still lives in the Pacific Northwest. Her favorite Christmas tradition is baking and, of course, eating Christmas cookies!